The Boy with the Blue Ears

The Boy with the Blue Ears

and 49 other Object Lessons for Children

Dorothy Brenner Francis

Abingdon
Nashville

THE BOY WITH THE BLUE EARS

Copyright © 1979 by Dorothy Brenner Francis

Library of Congress Cataloging in Publication Data

FRANCIS, DOROTHY BRENNER.
  The boy with the blue ears and 49 other object lessons
for children.
  1. Object-teaching.   2. Children's sermons.
  1. Title.
BV4315.F638   268'.432   79-9899

ISBN 0-687-03908-8

MANUFACTURED BY THE PARTHENON PRESS AT
NASHVILLE, TENNESSEE, UNITED STATES OF AMERICA

For Mary Quam

With warmest appreciation
for years of helpfulness at the
Marshalltown, Iowa, Public Library

CONTENTS

1-3-89

THE MAGIC NUMBER THREE

Prop: *A big number 3.*

Did you know that you can change a person's life by the things you say? It's true. You can. I first learned about this magic when I was in elementary school. I was about your age at the time, and I had a very wise teacher.

At the beginning of the school year this teacher asked the pupils in her class to introduce one another to her. Each child introduced the person sitting next to him. The only rule was that we had to tell three good things about the classmate we were introducing. Sounds crazy? Well, it wasn't crazy at all.

When you stop to consider, you can think of three good things to say about almost anyone, can't you? Sure you can. And that's the way it was with us back in my school days. Why, sometimes we mentioned good things about our neighbors that the neighbors themselves hadn't thought about at all.

I was really surprised when the boy sitting next to me told the teacher that I was always friendly to everyone. I hadn't thought much about my friendliness one way or the other until I heard my neighbor mention it. And immediately I

9

could think of several times when I hadn't been friendly at all.

I squirmed when I remembered how, that very morning, I hadn't spoken to an older man who was a friend of my father's. I knew the man, but I thought he wouldn't be interested in speaking to me, so I looked the other way. That wasn't being very friendly, was it?

The things my schoolmate told the teacher changed my life. He said I was friendly, so I tried to live up to his words. I went out of my way to smile at people and do small favors for them.

And people smiled back, and they went out of their way to help me. It was a chain reaction. I'm sure my teacher intended for this to happen. And the beauty of this story is that the idea still works. You can change a person's life by saying nice things about him when both he and others can hear.

The magic works best when you say three good things. Three seems to be a magic number. Who'd want to hear a story about Goldilocks and the four bears? And when fairy godmothers grant wishes, they always grant three of them, don't they? There is something satisfying about the number three. Experiment with it, and see what happens when you say three good things about your friend or your parents or your brothers and sisters.

Sentence prayer: Our Father, help us always to see the good in others and to let them know we see it. Amen.

IDEA MAN

Prop: *A paintbrush, some clothespins, and some cards.*

I don't usually brag about my relatives, but I want to tell you about my very bright nephew. Now Bill had an old-fashioned one-speed bike, while all the other kids on his block had fancy ten-speeds. Of course Bill wanted a ten-speed in the worst way, but he didn't have enough money to buy one. Bill had a paper route, but he had decided to save most of his paper-route money to help with college expenses later on.

When Bill saw the other kids riding their ten-speeds he was really tempted to use part of his college fund for a bike. But he fought that temptation. And he also began to wonder about his old bike. He used to like that bike just fine. It still took him almost everywhere he wanted to go around town. So Bill started to think of ways he could have fun with his old bike.

First, he painted it. And he painted it in his school colors. The paint job was such a success that he was invited to ride his bike in the homecoming parade.

To add a little more pizzazz, Bill threaded crepe paper in the school colors through the wheel spokes. Now he really looked fancy as he rode down the street.

Then someone showed Bill how to take small squares of cardboard and attach them to the spokes with clothespins in a way that made a snap-snapping noise when the wheels turned.

People in the neighborhood began to notice Bill. Several ladies hired him to run errands for them. The first thing he knew, he had another business in addition to his paper route.

The last time I heard from him, he had saved almost enough from his errand business to buy a ten-speed. But he wasn't sure he really wanted one, after all. He had had so much fun with the one-speed, he decided to keep it.

Well, I told you Bill was very bright. Sure, anyone could have thought of painting and decorating a bicycle. But I think it takes a lot of "smart" to be willing to try to turn a liability into an asset. Being willing is the big idea. That's why I'm thankful for Bill; he reminded me of this truth that I might otherwise have forgotten. It's sometimes good to be thankful for the unpleasant things in life, too.

We all have things in our lives that we would like to ditch for something better. Whatever our liabilities are, we can turn them into assets if we really try, and if we really want to. For this we should give thanks.

Sentence prayer: Our Father, help us to be thankful for our liabilities, knowing that if we try, we can turn them into assets. Amen.

HURRICANE

Prop: *A wind sock or a barometer.*

Scientists tell us that over all the earth an estimated 44,000 storms take place each day. This figure includes all kinds of storms—thunderstorms, tornadoes, cyclones, hurricanes. The atmosphere is very seldom calm and serene. But one of the most feared storms is the hurricane. Each year in the fall, weathermen start talking about the hurricane season.

Coastal areas are usually the areas hardest hit by hurricanes, and hurricane winds have such a great force that they can destroy everything in their path. These winds move in huge circular sweeps, yet at the center of this circle of wind, it is almost absolutely calm.

This calm place is called the eye of the storm. The winds nearest the center could be raging at 250 miles per hour, yet the center area would be calm. Sailors at sea have reported being completely surrounded by devastating winds, yet they were sailing on calm seas.

The eye of the hurricane is an amazing phenomenon, and there is a lesson to be learned from it, a comparison to be made, and a truth to discover.

We all experience storms in our own lives. And by this I do

not refer to thundershowers or blizzards or to any other of nature's storms. I'm talking about the stressful situations in our own lives. There are days when nothing seems to go right. We forget our lunch. We miss the school bus. We leave our homework on the kitchen table in our haste to get to school.

Or perhaps we are blamed for some unfortunate happening which was not our fault at all. Yes, storms frequently rage all around us. But there is a calm spot, and we can find it now that we know it is there.

The prophet Isaiah knew about this calm, and he said, "Thou wilt keep him in perfect peace, whose mind is stayed on thee" (Isaiah 26:3). What he was saying is that no matter how bad conditions around us become, we can find peace and calm if we think about God. God is the calm in the eye of human storms.

Try relaxing and thinking about God and his goodness the next time you feel life's storms raging around you. You may be amazed at what happens. The storm may not change, but by keeping calm and thinking of God for even a few moments, you are likely to find the strength and the wisdom to deal with your personal storm. Remember that although hurricanes rage, there is peace and calm in the eye of the storm.

Sentence prayer: Our Father, we thank you for the peace which surpasses all understanding. Amen.

LOVE THY NEIGHBOR

Prop: *A dictionary.*

The other day a young lady from the primary Sunday school class came to me with a problem. I was glad to talk with Mary, glad that she had chosen to come to me for help. This girl's problem was that she couldn't stand her work-partner at school. The teacher had assigned partners at the beginning of the term and Mary felt stuck for good.

When I asked Mary why she disliked her partner, she squirmed and blushed; then she said that her partner bragged and told lies, and that sometimes the partner made fun of her. I assumed that these things were true, at least from Mary's point of view, and I asked Mary why she hadn't discussed the problem with her teacher.

Mary said, "I learned at Sunday school that we're supposed to love our neighbors, but I don't even *like* this girl. I'd feel guilty complaining about her."

Now I was beginning to understand Mary's problem. I think we all know people whom we don't care for very much. Isn't that true? I think we all know people who rub us the wrong way for one reason or another. And it's always a problem to deal with these people. And we may become more confused than ever when we think of the words in the Bible that say we should love our neighbor as ourself.

But let's consider that. Now Mary told me she didn't love her partner. She even went farther than that, and said that she didn't even like her. Then I asked, "Do you hate her?"

Mary thought for a moment. "No," she said. "I don't really hate her. I'd just like to forget all about her."

I told Mary I didn't think that would work. Bothersome people seldom disappear from our lives. If we face facts, we know we're going to have to deal with them one way or another.

My suggestion to Mary was that she think about the difference between the words "love" and "like." So we looked them up in the dictionary. "Love" means to be concerned about a person, to have his good at heart. "Like" means to be pleased with someone.

Mary thought about that. Then she said, "You're saying I could be concerned for my partner without liking her, right?"

"Right," I said. "Even without liking her, you can be concerned about her, and maybe try to help her. Can you figure out why she brags and why she lies? Maybe she feels she's not as good as others and that she has to brag and lie to seem important. Maybe you can help her feel better about herself."

Mary agreed to try my idea, and I believe all of us could profit from thinking about the difference between loving and liking. Whenever you meet that person you can't stand, be concerned for him. You may be surprised at the results.

Sentence prayer: Our Father, help us to show loving concern for all our neighbors. Amen.

PEANUT BUTTER

Prop: *A new jar of peanut butter.*

At your house, do you ever fuss over who gets to take the first taste from a new jar of peanut butter? At my house, when I was growing up, we used to have a strict schedule for who got first dibs on the peanut butter.

I liked to take a fork and make criss-crosses in the smooth surface of a new jar of peanut butter before I took a taste. For some reason this gave me pleasure. My sister used to take a measuring spoon and scoop out little balls of peanut butter, leaving round holes in what remained. This pleased her. My older brother always dug into the peanut butter with a spatula, leaving a wide depression in the surface. That gave him enjoyment. But we all dug into that jar with enthusiasm.

Sometimes I like to compare a new day to a new jar of peanut butter. The nice thing is that we get a new day a lot more often than we get a new jar of peanut butter. Every twenty-four hours a new day is delivered to our doorstep to dig into as we please.

How we dig into a jar of peanut butter doesn't really affect the flavor of it, but the way we dig into a new day can definitely affect the flavor of those twenty-four hours.

17

Some people wait until the last possible minute, and then they drag themselves from bed reluctantly. They are behind schedule before they ever get a good start. And many times their lateness continues to hound them throughout the whole day. They have to gulp breakfast. Sometimes they have to wear mismatched clothes, because there's no time to hunt for the proper shirt, shoes, or socks. Then they miss the school bus.

Have these things ever happened to you? Then what? Someone may have to drive you to school, and it messes up that person's schedule. Or maybe you have to walk to school and are late for class. You may miss an important test or class discussion that will cause trouble for you the rest of the term.

How different the results are for the people who dig into the day with enthusiasm, determined to make the twenty-four hours count for something good. These people get up on time, eat and dress unhurriedly, catch the school bus with no trouble, and arrive for class with untroubled minds. These people are organized. Details of their lives vary, but the constant denominator is enthusiasm.

Anyone can organize his life if he wants to. Some people like to make out a list of things they hope to accomplish each day—a daily schedule which includes all the necessary things, along with plenty of other activities thrown in for some fun.

Tomorrow, remember this jar of peanut butter as you start a new day, and dig into it with enthusiasm.

Sentence prayer: Dear Father, help us dig into every day with enthusiasm and make each day count for something good. Amen.

HAPPINESS IS A FOOTBALL GAME

Prop: *A football helmet.*

When fall comes, can football be far behind? Most people like autumn with its crisp breezes and beautiful array of leaves. I think one of the most colorful pageants of the fall season is the football game. It's hard to resist the sound of the band, the sight of the cheerleaders in their bright costumes, the mingled smells of pom-pom mums and buttered popcorn.

For me, one of the puzzles of a football game is to figure out who has the ball, after it has been put into play. Twenty-two men are on the playing field. It's hard to watch twenty-two players all at once. And beside that, the players try to fool people. Oh, they aren't really trying to fool the spectators. The team with the ball tries to fool the members of the opposing team.

Each team has signals. When the quarterback calls a signal, his teammates know who is going to carry the ball. The other team and the spectators are sometimes fooled by the players who only pretend to have the ball. Many times a tackle will bring down a man who has nothing in his hands but air. It's really hard to know who has the ball.

And it's also hard to know who has the ball in the game of life. I sometimes think of happiness as representing the ball. Who has happiness? A lot of people pretend to have it. The kids who laugh at their parents and brag about staying up late to watch TV on school nights are pretending to have the ball. The next day when the teacher springs a test, they miss a lot of answers. Then you know all they had in their hands the night before was air.

And the boy who sneaks off the schoolground to spend his lunch money on candy and pop pretends to have the ball. But when the dentist checks for cavities and finds ten, you know that all that boy had in his hands was air. There are a lot of people who just pretend to have the ball.

Football is a tough game, and there are a lot of rules to follow. Each coach has a thick code book. And sometimes the rules keep changing from year to year, which makes the game even harder to play correctly.

We are lucky that the game of life isn't like football in that respect. In life's game we have just ten rules—the Ten Commandments. They aren't easy rules, but we can rest assured that they aren't going to be revised and presented in a new issue next year. They were standardized many centuries ago. If we study these ten rules and try to live by them, they will help us carry the ball, and they will help us recognize other people who are also carrying the ball. We won't be fooled by the pretenders quite so often.

Sentence prayer: Our Father, we thank you for rules to live by. Amen.

FAILURE

Prop: *A large report card with a red F on it.*

How many of you have ever failed at something? I would guess that almost every person living today has failed at something he tried to do. I know I have failed on several occasions. Sometimes people your age dread report-card time because there might be a failing grade on their record.

Failure is hard to take. It is hard to live with. When we fail at something, we feel inadequate and weak. And we may feel that the whole world is watching us—and laughing.

Failure is easier to live with if we stop to realize that it is a part of all human existence. All of us have failed and fallen short of our goals. God is the only one who is perfect. The important thing to learn from failure is that we must keep on trying.

How many important things can you name that were accomplished on the first try? Not many, that's for sure. Do you think that great athletes were great the first time they took part in their favorite sport? You know that's impossible, don't you? And the same thing is true of musicians. None of the greats learned to play overnight. It seems that way sometimes. Maybe all of a sudden you start hearing someone's name again and again. But if you check into that person's history, you will more than likely find that he was working toward his goal for years before he reached it, before you began hearing his name.

The TV singer who seems to be an overnight sensation probably put in years of work that went relatively unnoticed. The TV master of ceremonies whose name is now a household word may have worked for years for local stations where hardly anyone recognized his existence.

When we experience failure, we must try again. And if we fail again, we must try still one more time. The Old Testament of the Bible is filled with stories of failure followed by success. The children of Israel were held in bondage in Egypt through ten plagues. But Moses insisted that they keep trying to break free. The people gave up more than once, but Moses kept calling on them to try again. And at last, because they kept trying, and because they had faith in Moses and in God, they escaped from the Egyptians and into the Sinai desert.

If you have failed at something, don't let the failure cause you to give up. Reach for the hand of God, and defeat failure by trying again.

Sentence prayer: Our Father, help us to have the faith to try again—and again. Amen.

THE HELPING HAND

Prop: *A pebble.*

How many of you have ever had a pebble in your shoe? It's not very comfortable, is it? In fact, if the pebble is in just the wrong place, it hurts a lot. So what do you do? Sometimes when I get a pebble in my shoe, I hate to take time to remove it, so I limp around with it hurting me until the pain gets so bad I can't stand it. Do you ever do that? It's a silly thing to do, isn't it? Sooner or later the pebble has to come out.

Now let's think a bit about removing pebbles from shoes. What's hurting? Your foot, right? Can the foot remove its own shoe and toss away the pebble? This might be possible if you're wearing loafers. But if you're wearing a tie-shoe, your foot can't remove it. You have to use your hands, don't you?

Your hand helps your foot feel better, but your hand feels better too, doesn't it? Think about that. When you have a pebble in your shoe, your foot really hurts, but you're also miserable all over, aren't you? Nothing about you is very happy as long as that pebble is hurting you. So when your hand removes the pebble, both your foot and your hand feel better.

It might be interesting to think of the people of the world as the takers-out-of-pebbles. The world has a lot of pebbles that make it hurt. There are the pebbles of poverty, of hunger, and of war, just to name a few. The world is an unhappy place when the people in it are unhappy. And many times these people really can't help themselves. Poor people sometimes can do little to gain more material possessions. Hungry people, especially hungry children, can do little to bring more food into their homes. And the common people in war-torn countries can do little to bring peace.

What is the answer? Someone else must help. You must help. I must help. Perhaps there is little you and I can do to stop wars, but we can help fight global poverty and hunger. The pennies you give and collect for UNICEF go directly to fight hunger and poverty. That money tells the world that you care.

You can also help in the war on poverty and hunger here at home by making donations of food and gifts through your church at Thanksgiving and Christmas, and at any other time when a local need arises.

Remember the pebble in the shoe. The foot can't help itself, but the hand can help both the foot and itself. As we give, so shall we receive.

Sentence prayer: Our Father, help us to be aware of the needs of others, and create within us the desire to help. Amen.

V FOR VICTORY

Prop: *A duck decoy.*

On crisp fall mornings I like to watch the skies for formations of ducks flying south for the winter. Do you ever see ducks going south? Sometimes you can hear them before they come into view; then if you keep watching, you'll see their formation in the sky.

Does anyone know what that formation looks like? Right. It looks like a huge letter V. Now scientists haven't learned for sure how ducks know when it's time to fly south, and they don't know how these birds find their way to warmer climates, but the fact is that they do.

One thing scientists have learned is that the same bird does not always lead the formation at the point of the V. The ducks take turns. Leading the formation is very hard work, and scientists believe that the leader duck is helped along the way by the wind currents set up by all the fanning wings behind him. But being leader is still a tiring job, and after a while the leader lets another duck take over, while he drops back in the formation to be a follower.

Sometimes birds seem smarter than humans. How many of you know a leader? It could be a leader in games at school.

Or it could be the first person in the lunch line. Or maybe the first person to jump on the school bus in the afternoon. Life offers lots of opportunities for people to be leaders. But do you know some leaders who like being leaders so much they won't give other people a chance to lead?

And sometimes it's the same way with followers. A person may get so used to following that he never wants to take the responsibility for leading. Or maybe he has followed for so long that he is afraid he doesn't have the ability to lead.

Sometimes I think people should study the ways of ducks when it comes to leading and following. I think it's a good idea to take turns. If you've had a turn at leading, then take a turn at following. Or if you always seem to be a follower, work up your courage and take a turn at leading.

When you see a formation of ducks in the sky this fall, think about the letter V. Many years ago during World War II, when the great British leader Winston Churchill spoke to the allied troops, he raised two fingers to form the letter V. In those war-torn times everyone knew that V stood for just one word—victory. Could the ducks know this, too? Probably not, but I like to imagine they know that by taking turns leading and following, their flight will reach a victorious finish in a warm climate where they can survive for the winter.

This week, let's be at least as smart as the ducks. In our activities at home, at school, and at church, let's remember to take turns both leading and following.

Sentence prayer: Our Father, give us the wisdom to be both leaders and followers. Amen.

SECRETS

Prop: *A secret-code book.*

How many of you like secrets? Almost everyone likes a secret. When I was young I sent a cereal boxtop to a radio station to get a secret-code ring. I had a favorite mystery program, and each day the radio announcer gave clues to the mystery, but they were given in code. With my code ring I could figure out the clues. And of course I told my friends, and we all shared the secret.

But if you really like secrets, you can make your own. Did you every think about doing a good deed and keeping it a secret? It's a pleasant thing to do, and anyone can do it. Of course, it requires some thought.

What should you think about? Try thinking about someone you know who needs something you can give. For instance, think about snow. Do you know anyone on your block who has a hard time shoveling his sidewalk? Maybe there's an older person who can't get around as easily as most people. Or maybe there's someone who is sick and can't do such strenuous work.

If such a person lives in your neighborhood, you have a chance to do a good deed—secretly. It may take some planning. You may have to get up early and shovel that person's sidewalk before you go to school. Or maybe you could wait until dusk and slip over and do the shoveling just before dark.

Then comes the best part. You mustn't tell anyone what you have done. Well, maybe you could tell just one best friend. That way you can share the fun. But if you tell, you might want to make it on the condition that your friend do a secret good deed to tell you about.

There are many good deeds that can be done secretly. Who can think of some that you could do without anyone's knowing? (Give the children a chance to discuss this.)

Many of those are good suggestions. And here are some others. A garden could be weeded secretly, if you're sure you know the difference between a plant and a weed. A birdbath could be filled secretly. And a birdbath can be cleaned secretly. Sidewalks can be swept when nobody is looking. Toys can be picked up. A yard can be cleared of trash.

Whatever good deed you decide to do, try doing it secretly. Secrecy doubles the fun, and it can make you feel good all day long.

Sentence prayer: Our Father, thank you for our strong minds and bodies. Help us to use them for your good. Amen.

COURAGE FOR THE ASKING

Prop: *A backpack and a walking staff.*

I have a friend named Jack who is an avid backpacker. He has all sorts of fancy equipment, including an emergency kit that he carries on his back, as he walks miles and miles through the wilderness. Sometimes Jack hikes through mountains, sometimes through swamps. Many times he feels that he is walking where few other people have walked before, and this gives him a great thrill.

One time Jack was backpacking with a friend who was not as accomplished as he was. A storm was brewing behind them, and it was tornado season. Everything seemed to be working against them. They came to a roaring river, and there was no way to cross except by way of a railroad trestle. But they had to cross the river and reach safer ground before dark.

As they looked at the railroad trestle, Jack's friend panicked. I don't know how many of you have ever examined a railroad trestle closely, but it's not of solid construction like a bridge that carries cars. The railroad ties are spaced many inches apart, and there is nothing between those ties except space. A person walking across such a

29

bridge can look straight down at the water and rocks below, and this dizzying view panicked Jack's friend.

"I can't do it," he said.

But Jack kept calm. He looked his friend in the eye and asked, "Do you believe in God?"

"Yes, of course," the friend replied.

"Then trust him for the next ten minutes," Jack said. "Trust him to take care of you."

A remarkable change came over the friend then. He stood straight. He looked ahead instead of down. And he crossed the trestle without accident. His faith in God gave him courage in time of danger.

Today life is filled with many dangers—actual physical dangers. There is the danger of traffic. There is danger from people who may not have our best interests at heart. And there are dangers we bring on ourselves through our inexperience in life. Parents and teachers cannot always be with us to guard us from danger.

But God is always where we are. Whenever we are faced with danger, it will help to remember that God has always been with us, and that he won't desert us in time of need. If you find yourself in danger, don't panic. Instead, say a short prayer. Your prayer may consist of one word—HELP. But if you say it in a prayerful manner, and if you think positively that God is there and that he will help you, you will find the courage to face your danger. You may not be a backpacker with a lot of fancy equipment. But remember that everyone has an emergency kit in his mind. The name of the kit is prayer.

Sentence prayer: Our Father, we thank you for your saving presence. Amen.

CENTER STAGE

Prop: *A theater program.*

How many of you have ever attended a stage play in a real theater? I know you see lots of plays and movies on TV, but I'm talking about a real theater with a stage, with live actors, and with a curtain.

Those of you who have attended such a play will remember the magic moment when the curtain went up. Probably you arrived at the theater a bit ahead of curtain time, and maybe you were talking to the person next to you, or fidgeting with your program until the play began. But what happened when the curtain went up? Everything got quiet, didn't it? Everyone sat in silence waiting for the actors to tell them a story.

Sometimes playgoers find the theater so glamorous and attractive that they want to be on the stage too, and they go to school and study drama and voice, and maybe they do become actors. This is good. But what many people don't think about is the fact that all of us are actors every day of our lives.

Every morning when the sun rises, it is like the curtain going up on a new play. And this play can be the most exciting drama in the world, because we are the actors. We are the stars. We can write the script and create our own story to show the world.

Now you may be thinking that you have very little to say about how your day will be acted out. The alarm clock tells you to get up. Mom tells you to eat breakfast and get to school. Then teachers take over. You go to arithmetic class at a certain time, English class at another time. Lunch is scheduled for you; then you have afternoon classes. Who says we are writing the script and creating our own story?

Well, I say so because it's true. Have you ever heard of Shakespeare? You'll hear about him before you're through school. He was a great writer, and sometimes he wrote what we call sonnets. A sonnet is a poem constructed with exactly fourteen lines, and it has to have a certain rhyme pattern. But within those restrictions, the poet has a great deal of freedom.

Home schedules and school schedules are your restrictions, but as you work within them, you have to decide what your play will be. Isn't that true? You write the script and create the story of your life by your own actions. You can doze through classes, or you can pay attention and discover fascinating facts. You can daydream, or you can try your hand at doing something creative and interesting.

The story of your life is up to you. Think about this as you begin each new day. The curtain is going up. The audience is waiting to hear your story. What do you have to say?

Sentence prayer: Our Father, give us the wisdom to act out our lives for our own benefit, as well as that of others. Amen.

THE MENEHUNES (men-a-who-knees)

Prop: *A tiny doll or puppet.*

Years ago a race of little people called Menehunes lived in the Hawaiian islands. These people could build amazing things from lava rock in a single night, or so it was said. But the Menehunes were afraid of the huge Polynesians who shared their island.

Noko, the Menehune leader, was worried. One day a huge Polynesian sat down on a tuft of reeds. This wouldn't have been so important, except that the tuft of reeds was Noko's home. What to do! Noko decided to have a talk with Polynesian King Tomomo.

When Noko arrived at King Tomomo's palace he found the king catching fish, but he had no place to keep them. They were slipping back into the sea. Noko reached up and knocked on King Tomono's knee.

"I want to talk with you," he said.

The king shook his head. "I'm too busy," he said. "I'm keeping watch for enemies so I can warn my people of danger."

"I'll help you," Noko offered. "I can see farther than you can."

The king laughed at that, asking how a small one like Noko could see farther than a tall one like himself. Noko offered to make a deal with him.

"If I can prove that I can see a greater distance, will you grant me one wish?"

"Yes," the king agreed, "but if you can't see a greater distance, you and your people must leave the island forever."

"It's a deal," Noko said.

So the king stretched on tiptoe and said he could see palm trees on the next island. Then Noko took his turn. He climbed up King Tomono's leg, and from there to his shoulder, and from there to his head. With a foot on each of the king's ears, Noko peered into the distance.

"I see not only the palms on the distant island, but I can see beyond them to the beaches. No enemy is in sight."

The king knew he had been outsmarted, and he congratulated Noko. Then he ordered his people to take care that they never harm the Menehunes or their homes. Noko was so impressed with the king's kindness that he agreed to let the Polynesians rule the island by day, and the Menehunes would rule by night. When the moon rose, Noko and his people built a stone-walled pond in which the Hawaiians could keep the fish they caught, so they would always have a plentiful food supply.

From this folktale, we can see that it is possible for people who differ greatly from one another to get along together, by using the good each possesses for the benefit of the other. There are ways in which the strong can help the weak and ways in which the weak can help the strong. Whenever we get into disputes with our neighbors, let's remember the story of Noko and King Tomomo, and try to work out a friendly solution.

Sentence prayer: Our Father, help us to see the wisdom in helping one another. Amen.

STICKY TAPE

Prop: *A roll of Scotch tape.*

You all know what this is, don't you? Most of us use a lot of sticky tape at this time of year when we wrap our Christmas presents. It's simple to use. We just tear off a strip and press it onto the paper we want to hold together.

But have you ever put a piece of tape on a package and then realized you had forgotten to put something important inside the package? That's happened to most of us at some time or other.

What do we do then? We have to take the tape off. And we must be very careful. If we aren't careful, what will happen? So much of the Christmas wrap will stick to the tape that it will spoil the looks of the package. Whenever we put sticky tape on paper, some of the paper will stick to it.

Sometimes I think people are a lot like sticky tape. They stick to things, too. Think about yourselves. What do you stick to? You stick to your families, don't you? And you stick to your friends. And when you pull away from family and friends, some parts of them stick to you.

You pull away from your family every morning when you go to school, and whether you realize it or not, some of your family sticks to you. For instance, your manners are something you got from your family, and they stick to you, even when you've pulled away from home. At least your parents hope those manners stick to you. And for the most part they do. We all forget our good manners sometimes, but for the most part they stick to us.

And what about your friends? Ideas and habits that you learn from your friends stick to you, too. Maybe Suzie taught you to play jacks. Or maybe Dick taught you how to hold a football. The knowledge will stick with you for a long time.

Or maybe Mary always stops on the way to school and buys a candy bar at the corner grocery. That gives you the idea of doing it, too. And maybe that's not such a good idea. Ideas about eating and snacking have stuck to you from your family. So you have to make a decision. Who has the best idea, Mary or Mother?

Yes, people are a lot like sticky tape. We stick to them, and they stick to us, and when we separate, a part of each of us is attached to the other. For this reason we must take care to choose our friends carefully, and we must take care to be a good friend to others. If we do this, then we encourage an exchange of good things.

Sentence prayer: Our Father, give us wisdom in forming friendships that will enhance our lives and the lives of others. Amen.

SLIVERS

Prop: *A good-sized sliver of wood.*

How many of you have ever had a sliver in your finger? Most of you, I'd guess. Having a sliver is no fun, but now and then it happens. I can remember many years ago when I was visiting my grandparents. They had no wall-to-wall carpet, and upstairs, the bare hardwood floors were waxed to a high gloss.

One of my favorite pastimes was to kick off my shoes, take a running start, and slide in my stocking feet down the hallway. I'm sure my parents would have stopped me had they known what I was doing, but they were visiting downstairs.

I was having a grand time until I hit a rough spot on the floor and ran a splinter into my toe. Did that ever hurt! I jerked my sock off and pulled the splinter out, but the pain didn't stop. After a day or two, my toe was red and swollen. The pain grew so bad that I had to admit to my mother that I been floor-sliding at Grandma's.

The doctor verified what Mother feared. I had broken the sliver off, and the remaining portion was causing an infection in my toe. Well, the doctor removed the rest of the sliver, and in due time my toe healed.

Did you know that all splinters are not made of wood? And not all splinters get into hands and feet. Sometimes we can get splinters in our minds. These splinters may be in the form of unkind words spoken to us. Or they may be in the form of deeds that make us unhappy.

Unkind words and deeds can become slivers that fester in our minds and cause unpleasant reactions. If someone says something unkind to you, you may be tempted to say something unkind to the next person you meet. And how is that going to make you feel? Ashamed. Sad. Certainly not happy.

In some ways, splinters in the mind are like splinters in the toes. We have to remove them completely before healing can take place. We can remove a mind splinter by forgiving the person who caused the splinter. This may be easier said than done, but trying to understand the person who caused the splinter may help us.

Maybe someone called you a coward. Before you flare in anger, try to figure out why that person would say such a thing. Maybe he's scared of something that's about to happen. Maybe he thinks that by calling you a coward, he is showing how brave he is. If you can make that person feel better about himself, you will have accomplished two things. You will have helped him, and you will have removed a splinter from your own mind.

Try it and see. The next time you feel hurt, try making the person who caused your grief feel better about himself. You can remove a lot of splinters this way.

Sentence prayer: Our Father, help us to make other people feel good about themselves. Amen.

BANKING

Prop: *A penny bank.*

How many of you have penny banks at home? Most of us have had such banks at some time in our lives. One Christmas I received a penny bank, and I was really excited. I had watched my older brother hold his bank upside down and shake coins from it. Now I could do this, too. I turned the bank upside down and shook, but nothing came out. My brother laughed and told me I'd have to put something in the bank before I could shake anything out of it. I thought about this for a while and came to the conclusion that my brother was right. And I started saving my money.

Then one day when my penny bank was about full of coins, my father told me it was time to open the bank, count the money, and deposit it in a regular savings bank downtown. Well, I liked shaking the coins from my bank, but I had a lot of doubt about giving all the money to some stranger downtown. Dad explained to me how the system worked. He showed me his passbook which told how much money he had put in the bank in one column. Then in another column the book told how much money the bank had paid him for using his money. This was a new idea to me. I didn't know anyone would pay you for using your money. Now I was more interested.

We put my money in a savings account, and eventually, when I withdrew it, I had the original amount, plus some extra which the bank called interest.

My experience with the penny bank and the downtown bank taught me something. When I got to thinking about it, I could think of lots of different kinds of banks. For instance, there's a friendship bank. Now you may ask how you can put friendship into a bank. Well, really you can't. You have to put friendship into another person. But after you've deposited your friendship, you usually have a new friend, plus a lot of good times for interest.

Then there's the school bank. You put in some attention and hard work, and you can withdraw knowledge, plus good grades for interest.

When you get right down to it, almost everything in life is like a savings bank. You put something in, and you can take that something out, plus a lot more. You always win with an arrangement like that, and after you study the system, you'll realize that the more you put into life, the more you'll be able to take out.

Why not try an experiment this week? Really put yourself into everything you do. Give generously of your time and talents. I think you'll be surprised and pleased at the results.

Sentence prayer: Our Father, help us learn the wisdom of giving of ourselves. Amen.

CHRISTMAS PAST

Prop: *An old Christmas tree.*

Christmas trees can bring a lot of joy. It's fun to get all the family together and go pick out the tree. Sis wants a tall one that will touch the ceiling. Brother wants one with pine cones on it. Mom wants one that's fresh and green. Dad wants one with a straight trunk.

Then after the tree has been chosen and taken home, more fun is in the offing. It's fun to get out the decorations, to hang them on the tree, and to remember the first time they were used. And it's fun to make new decorations with which to remember the present year.

And of course it's pleasant to have the sight and smell and feel of the Christmas tree in the house during the holiday season. Some people feel that it isn't really Christmas until the tree is up.

But what happens after Christmas? Do you hate to take the tree down? Sometimes it's almost like parting with a friend. What becomes of that tree after the decorations have been removed? Sometimes if a live tree was purchased, it is planted outdoors. But then it's no longer a Christmas tree. It's a yard tree. And sometimes an old Christmas tree is hung with tidbits for the birds. But it no longer has the tinseled look of Christmas. In many towns the Scouts come around in trucks to pick up old Christmas trees, and the city holds a big bonfire.

It used to make me very sad to see a discarded Christmas tree. I saw it as a forgotten and forlorn thing. Then I had second thoughts on the matter. A Christmas tree serves its purpose at Christmas. How strange and out of place it would be to see a Christmas tree in the living room on Washington's birthday or on St. Patrick's Day or at Easter time.

A Christmas tree is for Christmastime. It is to remind us of the spirit of Christmas, of love, and peace, and goodwill toward men. After the Christmas season, the tree's job is over, and keeping the Christmas spirit alive is up to each one of us. The tree will have served a good purpose if it reminds us to love our neighbor, to keep the peace wherever we go, and to show goodwill to our fellow men.

So maybe we should have fewer regrets about taking the Christmas tree down. And maybe we should have more concern for our part in keeping the Christmas spirit alive through the fifty-one weeks until it is time to choose a new tree.

Sentence prayer: Our Father, help us keep the Christmas spirit alive the year round. Amen.

MAKE THAT POINT

Prop: *A miniature football goal.*

This is the time of year when we hear a lot about football bowl games. The Cotton Bowl, the Orange Bowl, the Rose Bowl. In those games the competition is tough, and every point counts. The fans cheer when their team scores a touchdown. Then usually there is a bit of silence before the chant goes up—MAKE THAT POINT! MAKE THAT POINT! When the ball sails between the goal posts, the crowd goes wild again. The cheerleaders shake their pom-poms. The band strikes up a tune. The touchdown has been topped off by the extra point!

Even people who don't follow football can learn a lot from the rules of the game. Everyday life is full of chances to make an extra point. Many times we see a chance, but we ignore it. Sometimes teachers will offer an extra point to those who read an extra chapter, or write an extra paper, or do an extra project. The chance for the extra point is there, and we have the choice of trying for it or ignoring it.

Sometimes you may have tried for an extra point and failed to make it. Nobody can win all the time, but there's an old saying that if you try for the moon and miss, you may catch a few stars by accident. Effort spent in trying for the best is seldom wasted.

If you try for the first team and don't make it, you may find that you'll have a better understanding of the game's fundamentals if you spend some time playing on the second team. And this knowledge will help you be a better player when you do make the first squad. Or maybe you're trying to sell the most cookies in your Scout troop. You may not win that honor, but it's a good guess that you will make new friends and gain new self-confidence for having used the opportunity to meet new people.

There are lots of chances for everyone to make extra points in life. You can make extra points by doing a little bit more than is required of you. If it's your turn to do the dishes, you can make an extra point with your parents by doing the dishes and taking out the garbage, as well. Try it. Someone will notice.

The outcome of a ball game can hang on the making of an extra point. Your life may not hang on that extra point, but if you try for those extras, you will find your days have been enriched as a result of the trying.

If you're making New Year's resolutions, add this one to your list. TRY FOR THE EXTRA POINTS IN LIFE.

Sentence prayer: Our Father, thank you for the opportunities all around us. Help us to see them and to use them. Amen.

BOWL GAMES

Prop: *A drum major's baton or a musical instrument.*

This is the time of year when many of us wish we had a ticket to a bowl game. Maybe we'd like to go to the Super Bowl. Many of us watch those big football games on TV, but not many of us are able to attend in person.

But whether we plan to watch a game from the living room or from the fifty-yard line, one of the favorite pregame festivities is the bowl parade. Dozens of bands gather from all parts of the nation to take part in these parades. Some of the bands are from high schools. Some are from colleges.

These bands are colorful, with each member dressed in a flashy uniform that may include things like white spats and gloves, or hats with tall feather plumes. And these bands make a lot of noise.

Many times as the bands wait for the parade to start, the individual members stand around and play on their instruments. A trombone player may show off some fancy slide work that sounds a lot like a bawling cow. A trumpet player may sound a bugle call, or maybe he'll play a brassy fanfare that blares above the other parade sounds. And the clarinet players! Several of them usually get together to see who can make the highest screech. Of course the tuba players are not to be outdone. They stand around umpah-umpahing for anyone who will listen.

All this noise can be nerve-racking, and the musicians, as well as the spectators, are impatient for the parade to begin. Once the magic moment arrives, the whole sound changes. The drum major takes his place at the front of the band. He blows a warning signal on his whistle, and the instruments become quiet.

The drum major gives a second signal, and the drums beat out a cadence. The band marches forward. At the next signal, the music begins. The instruments that produced only chaotic sounds before, now produce beautiful tunes. What a difference a drum major makes!

Sometimes I like to think that God is like a drum major. We all go around making our own noises and irritating other people, as well as ourselves, until we let him take charge and call the signals. Then, when we follow his lead, our lives take on direction and meaning, and everyone is happier.

This week, when you're tempted to do too much of your own thing, disregarding those around you, stop and listen for your drum major. He's there and he's waiting to be heard. Listen.

Sentence prayer: Our Father, thank you for the knowledge that you are always present and available to those who seek you. Amen.

THE BOY WITH THE BLUE EARS

Prop: *Earmuffs.*

Do you ever notice that some people complain a lot? You're probably not one of these people, but some folks complain about the weather or about their clothes or about their food or about their homes. Sometimes a little complaining is all right, provided a person follows the complaining with useful action. If there is something in your life that you don't like, it makes sense to ask yourself what you can do about it.

That is what Chester Greenwood did. How many of you have heard of Chester Greenwood? If you live in Farmington, Maine, you have probably heard of him, because Chester lived in that town over one hundred years ago. That's a long time ago, but people still remember him. And for good reason.

Now Maine is well known for its long, cold winters. Chester Greenwood liked winter. Winter is not what he complained about. And that's a good thing, too, because there's not a lot anyone can do about winter. What Chester did not like was for his ears to get cold. Chester liked to play outside in the winter, and he especially liked to ice-skate.

But when he stayed out ice-skating, his ears got so cold they turned blue. And then Chester complained. He told his parents that he couldn't go ice-skating with the other children because his ears turned blue.

Chester's father suggested that he pull his cap down over his ears.

"But it keeps slipping up," Chester said.

"Wrap a wool scarf around your ears," Mother said. "Tie it under your chin."

"A scarf wrapped around my ears makes them itch," Chester said.

Every time anyone made a suggestion, Chester had a reason why it wouldn't work. At last his mother grew tired of hearing him complain.

"Well," Mother said, "*I* can't think of anything else, so *you* better figure out something to keep your ears warm. If you don't, you'll be stuck inside all winter."

When Chester realized the problem had been dumped back into his own lap, he thought for a long time. At last he took two pieces of fur and stuck them on some wire. He bent the wire until it fitted over his head. He called his invention "ear-laps." Chester's grandmother helped by sewing the fur more securely onto the wires. Now Chester stopped complaining about blue ears. His ears stayed warm in spite of the cold weather.

In a few years Chester patented his ear-laps and opened a factory. It is said that he became the richest man in Farmington.

Whenever you're tempted to complain, first ask what *you* can do about the situation. The Creator has given each of you a brain, but it's up to you to use his gift.

Sentence prayer: Our Father, we thank you for our abilities. Amen.

POM-POM FEVER

Prop: *A cheerleader's pom-pom.*

I really like to see the pom-poms the cheerleaders use at basketball games. They are colorful, and there are so many of them that they are indeed eye-catching.

But I want to tell you what happened to me one time at a basketball game. I was in elementary school, and my favorite cousin was in high school. Hank was on the ball team, but he wasn't one of the starters. In fact, Hank was lucky if he got to play at all. But sometimes when the team was far enough ahead of its opponent, the coach would send Hank into the game.

Well, one game on our schedule was almost a sure thing. Two of the top players on the other team were benched with injuries, and our team was in tip-top shape. Hank told me he felt sure he would get to play, and I went to the gym early to be sure of getting a good seat.

Sure enough, in the third quarter the coach sent Hank onto the floor. And I didn't take my eyes off him until the cheerleaders stood up. They had worked out a fancy routine with their pom-poms that was so eye-catching I was watching it instead of what was going on in the game.

The next thing I knew, I heard the announcer say that Hank had scored a basket. I had missed the most important part of the game, as far as I was concerned. Hank had scored, and I had missed it.

In this case, my missing the action certainly didn't make a great deal of difference. Hank got to play awhile longer, and I saw him score his next shot. But the incident taught me a lesson.

I learned that it's easy to let the pom-poms in life get in the way of the main event. Maybe you intended to study your arithmetic, but some program on TV distracted you. And the next day you had a hard time on the arithmetic test. That TV program was like a pom-pom, wasn't it?

Life offers lots of pom-poms. Playing games with the gang might be a pom-pom that distracts you from doing your piano practice. Or reading a comic book might be the pom-pom that distracts you from cleaning your room. Can you think of other pom-poms that have distracted you?

We should remember that pom-poms aren't really bad in themselves. The ball games would be less colorful and less fun without the cheerleader's pom-poms, and life would be less colorful and less fun without TV and games and comic books. All these things have a place in our lives. But the important thing is to keep your mind on the things that are truly meaningful to you. Don't let pom-poms cause you to miss out on life's important events.

Sentence prayer: Our Father, help us to keep our lives balanced with both work and fun. Amen.

SNOWTIME

Prop: *A snow shovel.*

Sometimes people who work at radio and TV stations and at highway patrol offices don't look forward to the day after a big snow. Why? Because the telephones in these offices ring constantly as people call to ask one common question. Are the roads open?

If the roads are blocked, you may be glad, because it may mean that school is closed, and you'll have a holiday from classes. But after a very short time, most of us are eager to get back to our daily routines. We miss doing the things we usually do. And we quickly miss not being able to go places.

You can't get to grandma's house if the roads are closed, can you? You can't go to that out-of-town ball game if the highways are blocked. After a big snow, the city streets usually are cleared first. Then at least we can travel around town, go to the grocery store or the doctor's office. Then as more roads open, we have more choices of places to go.

Sometimes our minds are like closed roads. Did you ever think of that? For instance, if you dislike learning your spelling words, you are closing the road that leads to the enjoyment of reading and writing. If you refuse to learn arithmetic, you close many roads into the future. You close the road that might lead to a career in banking or engineering or chemical research.

The basic subjects you are expected to study in school today offer knowledge that will keep your roads to the future open. Maybe you don't like studying arithmetic or social studies. Everybody can't be expected to like every subject, but at least you can keep up with your assignments and not close the roads to your future.

You may ask, "Who can predict what the future may be?" And of course, nobody can answer that for sure. But you children today are growing up in an interdependent kind of global community. Do you know what that means? It means that people from all lands in the world are realizing that they must work together if they are to survive.

When you are grown, the world will be much different from the way it is today. You can depend on that. And since nobody knows exactly how it will be different, the only wise thing to do is to keep as many channels to the future open as you can. A closed mind is a lot like a closed road. You can't go anywhere on it.

Sentence prayer: Our Father, thank you for our minds. Help us to keep them open for our own good and for the good of the world. Amen.

THOSE RED-LETTER DAYS

Prop: *A calendar with the holidays in red.*

All the days on the calendar look very much alike, don't they? There are only a few that are printed in red. Do you know why? Those red-letter days are special holidays. But for the most part the calendar days look very much alike. Common days. But if you get down to the truth of the matter, each person decides whether his day will be common or special.

If you wake up in the morning and tell yourself that this day is going to be special, chances are it will be special. But it's up to you.

Do you know the poem "Mary Had a Little Lamb"? Your mothers probably told it to you before you knew how to read.

> Mary had a little lamb;
> Its fleece was white as snow,
> And everywhere that Mary went,
> The lamb was sure to go.

Do you know who wrote those lines? The poem was written over 150 years ago. The special thing about it is that it was written by an ordinary thirteen-year-old boy named John Roulstone. He got his idea from an ordinary day at his ordinary school in Sterling, Massachusetts.

One hundred fifty years ago some children went to classes in one-room schools. Sometimes they walked long distances to get to school, and sometimes their pets followed them. Did you ever have a dog or cat follow you to school? If you live close to school you can take the pet home, can't you?

Well, on a common day 150 years ago a pet lamb followed a girl named Mary Sawyer to school. Mary had walked too far to take the lamb home, so it had to stay at school. And the lamb was so playful that it distracted the children from their lessons, so the teacher shut it in a shed. This was a common thing to do. It kept the pet safe, and it allowed classes to continue.

But that night after John Roulstone got home from school, he thought about the lamb following Mary. John decided to do something special, and he wrote the "Mary Had a Little Lamb" poem. It is not known for sure how the poem happened to become famous. But we can guess that John's mother showed it to a neighbor. Mothers do things like that. Maybe she showed it to John's teacher. Anyway, the poem was published, and today the poem is considered a contribution to our way of life. One common boy took a common happening from a common day and turned it into something special.

We all may not be able to write a poem or sing a song or paint a picture. But on each common day, each of us can do something special to make those around us happy. Name some ways you can make others happy. (Let the children talk.) You might want to try an experiment. Every time you do something special for someone, mark that day in red on your calendar. At the end of the week, count the red marks. See how may common days you turned into special days.

Sentence prayer: Our Father, help us to make every day a special day in your sight. Amen.

THE TOOTHPEST

Prop: *A tube of toothpaste.*

I once heard a poem about toothpaste that went:

> I'd really like to tell the chap off
> Who squeezes last, then leaves the cap off.

Does that ever happen at your house? Does someone use the toothpaste and then leave the cap off? It happens at my house now and then, and we have toothpaste all over everything if we aren't careful.

How many of you like to brush your teeth? The toothpaste has a nice fresh taste, and it's really a lot of fun to squeeze it from the tube. It comes out in a nice, flowing cylinder. Sometimes it's white. But it may be pink or green or blue or maybe even striped.

But there's one drawback to using toothpaste. If you squeeze too much from the tube, there's no way you can put it back. Have you ever tried to put toothpaste back into the tube? Impossible.

In a way, toothpaste is a lot like words. Words are other things that can't be put back once they are out. Now too much toothpaste may get mashed into the carpet and make a mess. Or it may be smeared around the lavatory and look terrible. But toothpaste usually doesn't do much real harm. It can be cleaned up, and other than the waste, not much damage will result.

But words are another matter. Words spoken in anger can hurt people. Words spoken carelessly can change another's life for the worse. I once knew a boy who called his little brother "dummy" quite frequently. And the younger boy didn't seem too bright in school. However, tests showed that he was bright enough. He just never lived up to his test scores. I always wondered if his brother had called him a dummy for so long that he actually believed that he was dumb.

Now I'm sure you do not call one another dummies, but sometimes words slip out accidentally. Most of us can have very bad accidents with words when we are angry. We may say things like, "I hate you," or "I wish you were dead," or "Go away and leave me alone." We may say these things to people we like very much. And after we cool down we are sorry for our words. But it's too late then. The words are out, and they can't be put back.

Oh, we can apologize for hard words, and we should do that. But the real damage has been done. It's a lot better to treat words like toothpaste—keep a cap handy, and use it before it's too late.

Sentence prayer: Our Father, help us all to think before we speak. Amen.

YOUR FRAME OF MIND

Prop: *An empty picture frame.*

How many of you know what this is? Of course. It's a picture frame. But the different thing about it is that it has no picture inside. In a way, that is sort of nice. When a picture frame is empty, then a person can put any picture he likes in it.

Have you ever bought a picture frame at the dime store? Picture frames in dime stores sometimes have pictures in them. It might be a picture of a movie star or some person you don't know. Sometimes I buy antique picture frames at auction sales or in an antique shop. These usually have pictures in them that I don't care for. So I take out these pictures and put in pictures I like. That's the nice thing about picture frames, you can decide what goes inside them.

Have you ever heard the expression "frame of mind"? Sometimes you may have heard someone say of someone else, "He's not in a very good frame of mind right now." Do you know what this expression means? It means the person is not in a very good mood.

It is interesting to think of "frame of mind" as putting a frame around your thoughts. How would your thoughts

60

look if they were put in this frame for everyone to see? Would the picture be pretty, or would it be ugly?

Of course your frame of mind changes from time to time during a day. What is your mood when your mother wakes you in the morning? Maybe not so good. But the choice of thoughts is up to each of us. We can hate to get out of bed. Or we can look forward to the exciting things the day holds in store. Our choice determines the picture that would appear in our mind-frame.

If you were to make a list of pleasant thoughts that would look nice in your mind-frame, what would some of your choices be? (Let the children name choices.)

One way to make good choices about your thoughts is to try to think as Jesus might think—thoughts of love, joy, peace. Of course this is not always easy, and sometimes it is extremely hard. But the first step to take in determining your frame of mind is to be conscious of your thoughts.

Catch yourself, when you find yourself thinking unpleasant thoughts. Imagine how those thoughts would look in a frame, and then change them to thoughts worthy of framing.

Sentence prayer: Our Father, help us realize that our thoughts help determine our happiness. Keep us in the proper frame of mind. Amen.

THAT SPECIAL PURR

Prop: *A picture of a cat.*

I once went with a girl to the pet shop to pick out a pet cat. When we arrived at the shop there were several kinds of cats on display. But this child almost immediately was attracted to a rather scrawny short-haired cat that seemed completely unremarkable to me.

"Look, Suzie," I said. "See the pretty Persian cat. See how it fluffs its long hair."

"It's nice," Suzie said. But she went right on holding the scrawny short-haired cat, petting it, pressing her cheek to it.

"Did you see this Siamese?" I asked. "Look how still he can stand. Why, he looks almost like a statue."

Suzie eyed the Siamese and nodded, "It's nice." But she went right on holding the scrawny, short-haired cat, stroking it and scratching it behind its ears.

Then I pointed out another cat to her. "See the calico," I said, "I'll bet that one is a good mouser. See how his tail twitches."

Again Suzie nodded, "The calico is nice. And so are the Persian and the Siamese. But this cat is the one I want."

"Why, Suzie?" I asked.

"I like the way it purrs," Suzie said.

"But all cats purr," I argued. "You might as well pick a pretty one."

"I know they all purr," Suzie said, "But this one has a special purr. Hear it?"

There was no use discussing the matter any more. Suzie had made her choice. And I think there is something to be learned from her choice. We hear a lot these days about doing our own thing, about making the most of our individual talents.

Suzie's cat made the most of a very small talent—purring. All cats purr, but Suzie's cat had a special purr—at least for Suzie.

Sometimes people become discouraged with the talents they possess. In fact, some people may think they don't have any talent at all. Sometimes we grow up thinking that our older sister or brother has all the talent in the family, just because he or she is older and stronger and has had a bit more experience in the world.

Or sometimes we look at movie and TV stars and think they have all the talent in the world. Suzie's choice of cats proves that "it ain't necessarily so." Nobody has dibs on the talent market. Our talents are what we make of them. Even small talents can be used in a way that makes them special to someone. I try to keep this in mind on days when my life seems to be in a rut—days when things seem to go wrong. I try to remember Suzie's cat, and that usually inspires me to keep on doing my thing in my own special way.

Sentence prayer: Our Father, help us to be aware of the many talents you have bestowed upon us. Amen.

FRIED CAKES AND SAILING SHIPS

Prop: *A doughnut.*

The Bible tells us that faith is the assurance of things hoped for. What do you think that means? Could it mean that if you hope for a good thing and have faith that you will receive that thing, you will receive it? Evidence points in that direction.

For example, consider the experience of Hanson Gregory. Hanson lived about 125 years ago in New England. He lived along the seacoast, and each day he watched ships coming and going in the harbor. Hanson wanted to be a seaman. That was one of the things he hoped for.

Another thing Hanson hoped for was not to have to eat any more of his mother's fried cakes for breakfast. Like most mothers, Hanson's mother believed that everyone should start the day by eating a good breakfast. She was an excellent cook and sometimes she made fried cakes for breakfast. Her feelings were hurt when Hanson refused to eat them.

"Why don't you want any cakes?" Mrs. Gregory asked.

"I like your cooking, Mother," Hanson said. "But those breakfast cakes are soggy in the middle. They lie in my stomach like bricks."

"Hanson!" Clearly, Mrs. Gregory's feelings were hurt.

Now Hanson hadn't intended to hurt his mother's feelings. He just wanted to protect his stomach. How could he keep both his mother and his stomach happy?

Hanson liked the edges of his mother's cakes. The edges were light and delicious. He thought about that and then he had an idea. And Hanson was willing to work for his idea.

The next time his family had fried cakes for breakfast, Hanson's mother allowed him to cook them. He took some of the unfried cakes and cut the centers from them. Then he fried them as his mother usually did. The unused centers were kneaded together to make more cakes. And his idea worked! The soggy centers were no more, and the outer rings of cake were delicious. Hanson didn't know it then, but he had just invented the doughnut. Hanson's faith helped him get what he had hoped for.

But Hanson was not really interested in the doughnut business. The big thing he hoped for was to be a sea captain. Again he had faith. And again he backed his faith with work. He went to sea as a cabin boy. A few years later his work and faith paid off, and he became the skipper of his own ship.

Before a person can have anything, he must have a clear picture of it in his mind. And he must believe that having the hoped-for thing is possible. Thomas Jefferson hoped for a tool that would turn an unbroken furrow of earth. Work and faith brought about the plow. Alexander Bell hoped for an instrument that would enable men to talk to each other when they were far apart. Faith and work brought the telephone into being.

What good thing do you hope for?

Sentence prayer: Our Father, help us to be strong in our faith. Amen.

WHAT'S IN A NAME?

Prop: *A nametag for each child.*

Your name is a most important thing. A name is just a word or two, but it is the word or two the world knows you by. I have a friend who I sometimes think is wise beyond his years. When he was very young, he seemed to know the importance of a name. Now this young friend, Bill Jackson, owned a rabbit. Bill lived in town, and his home was on a very small plot of ground. But there was enough grass and clover growing on that plot of ground to feed his rabbit, and he gathered the greenery each day for his pet.

Then one day when Bill went to the rabbit pen, he found a big surprise. There was his rabbit—with ten babies. Bill went running to tell his parents. He was surprised that they weren't as excited about the ten babies as he was.

"You'll have to give them away, Bill," Dad said. "This yard has only enough grass for one rabbit."

Well, Bill did not give up. When the rabbits were old enough to eat greenery, he spent his allowance on lettuce, but he couldn't keep up with the rabbits' appetites. Then he hit on another idea. He invited ten friends to come see his rabbits. And he offered to name a rabbit after each friend who would bring enough grass and clover each day to feed one rabbit. The plan worked.

All Bill's friends were eager to have rabbits named after them, so they brought greens for their namesakes. Bill got to keep the rabbits, which made him happy, and his friends had rabbits named after them, which made them happy.

Bill succeeded in keeping his rabbits, at least for a while, because he knew the importance of a name. He knew that people like to be proud of their names. Names are important, and we should always remember that fact, and never do anything that would bring discredit to our names.

Life offers a lot of temptations. Almost every day we may be tempted to cheat or to lie or to steal. Often it's hard to do the right thing. But many times it will help us to make the right decision if we think about what our actions will do to our good names.

Do we want to be known as cheaters or liars or thieves? Of course not. Our names are the way the world knows us. If we remember this, it will make doing the right thing much easier. This next week, whenever you are tempted to do something you know is not quite right, say your full name over to yourself five times. And remember that what you do reflects on that name. The world knows you by your name.

Sentence prayer: Our Father, we thank you for our good names and ask your help in keeping them untarnished. Amen.

THE PRIZE

Prop: *A box of cereal and samples of cereal prizes.*

How many of you choose your breakfast cereal according to the prize that is to be found within the package? All of us have probably done this at some time in our lives. The prize may be a whistle or a bag of marbles or a toy model of some sort.

Sometimes I used to spend a long time in the cereal aisle at the grocery store just trying to figure out which cereal package offered the best prize. Then when we got home with the groceries, Mother always announced that I had to eat the cereal before I could have the prize. I thought this rule unfair, because my buddy next door got to dig right into the cereal box and pull out the prize first thing. Then sometimes he didn't even eat the Crunchie-munchies or the Toastie-woasties. But none of that business for *my* mother. I ate the cereal first, or no prize.

But when I finally found the prize, I opened it, played with it briefly, then raced from the house to show it to my friends. I had earned the prize, and somehow the things a person earns are more meaningful than things that come too easily.

I often think that each day of our lives is like a package of cereal in many respects. We have to work our way through it to the prize. Only a day is much better than a package of cereal, if you consider that a day may offer several prizes, and cereal usually offers just one.

It's true that we have to work our way through our daily chores—making beds, picking up things in our room, helping around the house. We have to work through the rest of the day at school, and then maybe there's a music lesson that has to be practiced and homework that has to be done.

But at bedtime it's good to stop and consider what the prizes for the day were. Maybe the teacher chose your spelling paper to display on the bulletin board. That's a prize. Or maybe you saw the first robin so far this spring. That's another prize. Or maybe the tulip bulbs you planted long ago last fall poked through the ground at last. That's another prize.

Prizes come in all sizes and shapes. And some prizes come in the form of words. Maybe someone looks at you and says, "You did a good job." That's another real prize.

But whatever happens during a day, you can usually find some prizes if you stop and think. Bright spots stand out—spots that make the whole day worthwhile. So each night before you fall asleep, think back over your day and ask yourself, "What was the prize?"

Sentence prayer: Our Father, help us to be thankful for the good to be found in each day. Amen.

THE WISE FOOL

Prop: *A court jester's cap or slippers.*

In olden times, in the days of kings and queens and kingdoms, and before the days of TV and radio and movies, people called court jesters were the chief entertainers of the world. Each king had at least one court jester, and perhaps, if he were a very rich king, he had several jesters to keep him entertained. Sometimes these jesters were called fools.

The court fool's job was to tell stories and jokes or do tricks for the amusement of the king. Now once there was a court fool named Jewel. All his life Jewel had performed for kings and queens and told them stories and jokes, but Jewel was not a good fool, because he sometimes forgot the ends of his jokes. He could not remember the punch lines.

Well, needless to say, this made the kings and queens very angry. Fool Jewel lost one job after another and had to wander from castle to castle trying to find work. The knights who guarded the castle walls all recognized Jewel, and they would laugh and tell him to wait his turn, but not to expect a job.

Well, finally Jewel had an idea. He knew he couldn't remember his jokes, so the next time he went before a king he said, "Your Highness, tell me, what kind of jokes do you like?"

This surprised the king, but it made him think. At last he began telling the sort of joke he liked.

The king told one joke, and then he smiled. He told a second joke, and then he smiled and slapped his knee. After he told a third joke, he smiled, slapped his knee, and laughed right out loud. The king was so happy he spent the rest of the day telling jokes to Fool Jewel. And when at last he finished, the king called his knights to him and said, "I have hired Fool Jewel as my court jester. Show him to his royal quarters. Serve him a royal dinner. And bring him to me first thing tomorrow morning."

The knights were surprised, but they followed the king's orders. And from that day on, Jewel had a secure job, and the king became his true friend.

Fool Jewel really wasn't a fool at all. He learned that one sure way to make friends is to listen to what the other person has to say. Nobody expects anyone to listen all the time, but too many of us are all talk and no listen. Whenever I find myself talking too much, I remember the story of Fool Jewel and I lend an ear instead of a tongue. Let's all remind ourselves to listen to other people this coming week and see what a difference it can make in our lives.

Sentence prayer: Our Father, thank you that we have ears as well as tongues, and help us put both to the best use possible. Amen.

THE SPOTLIGHT

Prop: *Some pictures of currently famous people.*

How many of these people do you recognize? (Hold the pictures up one at a time and wait for answers.) Yes, most of these people are so well known that everyone recognizes them and knows at least a little about why they are famous.

Have you ever thought about being famous? Most of us think about it, at least fleetingly, at some time in our lives. And most of us think it would be fun to be famous and have everyone in the nation recognize our picture and know what we have done to earn the fame.

The dream of fame is all right if you are willing to work to earn it. I have a feeling that most of these famous people had goals they worked toward, and that after they achieved their goals, the fame came—a result of their hard work.

Of course, everyone who works hard will not become famous. Many people work hard every day of their lives, and they are known only to their families and friends. And while many people who achieve fame have worked hard, at least some of them hired publicity agents to assure their fame.

Do you know what a publicity agent is? That's a person

who's paid to see that a certain person gets his picture in the paper or gets a spot on a popular TV show or has his name mentioned by a certain news columnist. Somehow fame doesn't seem like so much fun when you know a person paid to get it.

Centuries ago a wise Chinese man said, "Sorrow not that men do not know you, but sorrow that you do not know man." Ancient wise men sometimes were hard to understand. This man was saying that we shouldn't be concerned because we aren't famous, but we should be concerned because we don't recognize the fame or the good in the people around us, and because we don't understand others.

We can learn a lot from the people around us. Every person has worthwhile talents, and we enrich our own lives when we recognize the talents of the other people.

Another thing we can do to make the world a happier place is to point out the talents of others. Everyone needs a publicity agent of the volunteer sort. Notice the people around you this coming week. If you think someone is doing a really good job at something, tell others about it. Everyone likes to be recognized for the things he or she does well, and we miss out on a lot when we let these well-done things go unnoticed.

So look around you every day. Pay attention to others and to the good things they are doing. The attention you give to the deeds of others will enrich your own life.

Sentence prayer: Our Father, help us always to see the good in our friends and to be enriched by it. Amen.

THAT SPECIAL TALENT

Prop: *A baseball.*

How many of you like to play baseball or watch baseball games? Almost everyone likes baseball, but not everyone can play the game well. I want to tell you about a neighbor of mine, Jim. Jim is a boy about your age, and he wanted to be on the Little League team in the worst way, but he just couldn't quite make it. Jim wasn't a good pitcher, and his hands were too small for catching. When he was up to bat he never hit a ball very far, and when he ran he was usually too slow. Sometimes Jim wanted to quit trying to play baseball, but his dad wouldn't let him give up.

Jim's dad told him that in order to make himself valuable to a team, he must develop a specialty that none of the other team members had. What specialty could he develop? Jim couldn't think of any. But his dad took him to some ball games and told him to watch carefully. At last Jim noticed a kind of batting that he thought he could learn to do. Bunting.

Jim noticed that when a hitter bunted the ball, he might be put out, but it usually allowed another player to make it to the next base. Jim's dad showed him how to hold the bat, and

Jim practiced bunting every evening. After several weeks he was becoming a good bunter. He could bunt to the left or to the right or straight ahead. Jim had developed a talent that was different and valuable, and he not only made the team, he got to play in almost every game.

The truth is that we all have special talents we can develop that will get us where we want to go. We all can't be fast runners or eagle-eye pitchers. We all can't be champions at math or key musicians. But we all have some talent that we can develop to make ourselves useful to the world, and as a consequence, we can make ourselves happier persons.

Sometimes we may have a hard time realizing what our special talents are. We may have to watch and learn from others who are older and wiser than we are. And we may have to spend hours and hours practicing to develop whatever talents we may find within ourselves. But the time and effort are well worth the struggle.

This week, why doesn't each of you take a long, hard look at your life, and see what potential talents you can find to use for your own benefit, as well as for the benefit of those around you.

Sentence prayer: Our Father, we thank you for so generously giving us the talents we need to live in your world. Help us to develop them in the best way possible. Amen.

THE CHERRY TREE

Prop: *A small potted tree.*

Have you ever noticed how long it takes a tree to grow? Sometimes in a magazine or newspaper advertisement, you'll see a picture of a beautiful tree, fully grown and in bloom. The ad says you can buy such a tree for just a few dollars. But when you get to the nursery and the salesperson shows you the tree, you can hardly believe it's the same tree that was advertised in the picture.

Of course the salesperson explains that the picture in the ad showed the tree as it will be when it's full-grown. Sometimes it takes a lot of imagination to imagine the little shrub of roots and limbs that you buy as a big tree, full-limbed, and shading your backyard patio.

I bought a small tree like that once, a cherry tree. Of course I tried to imagine it as fully grown and bearing delicious cherries. But when I looked at the tree, all I could see was a spindly trunk and some scraggly limbs with only a few leaves. My tree looked like something a comic artist might have drawn as a cartoon.

This tree was right outside my kitchen window where I saw it many times each day. Maybe looking at it so often made the growth rate seem even slower. Sometimes that's the case. But one day when I looked at the tree I saw a robin sitting on one of the tiny branches, one small robin. The branch bent under the weight of the bird, but it didn't break. It held the robin, and the robin seemed pleased. At least it was singing as if it were pleased.

Then the next thing I knew, two robins were building a nest in that little cherry tree, right where the limb joined the spindly trunk. As the days passed, I watched the nest grow. Then presently I saw three blue eggs in the nest. And not long after that, I saw three baby birds with their mouths wide open, waiting to be fed.

Gradually I began to have a lot of respect for that little cherry tree. It certainly wasn't anything like the picture in the ad, but it had been useful. It had provided a home for a family of robins. It had done what it was able to do.

I think we can all learn from that cherry tree. We're all in the process of growing. You children have a lot of physical growing to do, and we adults still have a lot of mental growing to do. But along the way, we can be like that cherry tree. We can be useful. We can do what we are able to do at our present stage of growth.

Sentence prayer: Our Father, we thank you that we all can be useful in your wonderful world. Amen.

KNUCKLES DOWN

Prop: *A bag of marbles.*

Many people think that the robin is the first sign of spring, but many schoolteachers and parents feel that a child with a bag of marbles is really the first indication that winter is over. How many of you like to play marbles? How many of you collect marbles?

Marbles is a very old game. There were people who lived in America even before the Indians, and they were called Mound Builders. There is evidence that those people played marbles. Some of their marbles were made of flint, and others were made of clay. Some of them were even chipped from other kinds of stone.

Children of old Egypt played marbles, and so did children of ancient Rome. And Chinese children have played marbles for over five thousand years.

Long ago, English choir boys played marbles. England has a very famous church which is called Westminster Abbey, and choir boys played marbles on the abbey steps, even before Columbus discovered America.

In England, adults also played marbles. It was actually a grownups' game, and they made many rules. A player could not lift his shooter. A player had to shoot with "knuckles down."

Presidents have played marbles, and kings have played marbles. Playing marbles is a fine sport, and collecting marbles is a fine hobby.

I believe that anything that lasts a very long time must be worthwhile. For instance, I think the game of marbles has lasted through many centuries because it is good fun, and also because it has something to teach us. Can you think of some things you have learned from playing marbles? Maybe you've learned to enjoy the beauty of marbles. There are so many kinds, and they are all useful. Maybe you've learned to play fair with your friends by playing marbles. Maybe you've learned that playing goes smoothly when you keep the rules of the game, and that the game goes poorly when a player breaks the rules.

In this way the game of marbles is a lot like the game of life. We enjoy life a lot more when we learn to enjoy people. There are many kinds of people, and all kinds are different, and all kinds are useful. And maybe you've noticed that the game of life goes more smoothly when you keep the rules. The Ten Commandments are the basic rules, and when you break one of them, it slows the game of life down in many ways.

This week, as you play marbles on the playground or in your own backyard, enjoy the beauty of the game, and keep the rules. It's good practice for the game of life.

Sentence prayer: Our Father, give us the strength and the wisdom to play fair on our way through life. Amen.

TROUBLESHOOTER

Prop: *A puzzle.*

How many of you like to work puzzles? Most of you, I'd guess. And most of you have good ideas when it comes to figuring what to do in a tough situation. Did you know that sometimes you have better ideas than grownups do? That is true—sometimes.

I once read about a truck driver who got his huge truck stuck under an overpass. There the truck sat, and it was about an inch too high to pass safely under the overhead bridge. Alternate highways were miles out of the way, and the cargo in the truck was perishable. It had to be delivered on time.

The police stood around wondering what to do. The truck driver stood there wondering what to do. Motorists sat in the cars and honked their horns, irritated at the delay. But at last a small boy who had been watching spoke up.

"If you let some air out of the tires, it would lower the truck enough to get it under the bridge."

Silence. Everyone looked at this kid for a moment, and then they grinned. It was a good idea. The driver released some air from all the tires, and then he managed to drive his truck right under the overpass.

And one time when I was small, I was out riding with my parents on a snow-packed road. Our car stalled on a slippery hill. Dad got out and tried to push the car while Mom guided it, but that didn't work. Then all three of us tried to shovel sand under the wheels. That didn't work either. Dad was blaming himself for not having the gas tank filled. He said that a full tank of gasoline would give the weight needed to provide traction for the rear wheels.

At last Dad and Mom sat in the car, hoping that a passing motorist would stop and then send help to us from the nearest service station. I got tired waiting, so I got out of the car and began building a snowman. When I was ready to put the huge snowballs together, I had an idea. Those big snowballs were heavy. Why not put them in the car trunk? Surely they would weigh as much as a tankful of gasoline.

Dad liked my idea, and together we heaved the parts of my almost-a-snowman into the trunk of the car. This time when we tried to go up the hill, the rear wheels caught hold, and we were unstuck.

All families have problems in the course of daily living, and sometimes children don't try to help solve those problems, because they think it's strictly a job for adults. Not so. Whatever problem you or your family face, do your best to help solve it. You may not always come up with the right answer, but sometimes you will. And those are the times that count.

Sentence prayer: Our Father, help us to have confidence in our own abilities and to use them for good. Amen.

THE RUNAWAY

Prop: *A roadmap.*

We read a lot in the papers today about children who run away. Maybe everyone thinks about running away at some time during his life. Have any of you ever thought about running away?

I can remember the story about one little boy who was standing at the corner just down the street from the house where he lived. A neighbor came by and asked him what he was doing, and he said he was running away from home. The neighbor commented that he hadn't gone very far, to which the child replied, "I've gone as far as I can go. I'm not allowed to cross the street, you know."

But sometimes children run farther away from home than the nearest corner. I had a friend who ran away. I don't remember now what his reasons were, but he came from a large family and things weren't going to suit him, so he packed a few things in a small suitcase and took off. Now he really expected someone to come after him. But nobody did. At last it began to get dark, and there he was without any place to sleep, and so far nobody had come hunting for him.

My friend crept back home and peeked through the window. There was his family, gathered around the supper table. His place was set, but his brothers and sisters were eating his share of food. They didn't seem to miss him! Well, he faced a decision. Did he want to spend the night out in the dark all alone, or did he want to return to the family circle where there was a place for him? You can probably guess that he returned to his family, and that experience cured him of running away.

I can remember once having a puppy that ran away from home. We were trying to train it, and everything was going wrong. The puppy had drunk water from the aquarium. He had left nose marks on my mother's windows. And he had smashed a vase on an end table when he wagged his tail.

We swatted him with a newspaper, and he took off. Later I found him in a nearby park. He drank from the lagoon, then he left nose prints on the shelter-house windows. But nobody cared. I watched him from a distance as he slunk back home.

When he was welcomed with pats and hugs, he perked up. I think he learned a lesson. I think he learned that he'd rather live with a few rules and be around people who cared for him, than to have his own way about everything and be all alone. What do you think?

Sentence prayer: Dear Father, help us to remember that rules usually mean love. Amen.

THE GUMBALL MACHINE

Prop: *A gumball or a toy gumball machine.*

The first time I saw a gumball machine, I really was fascinated. Here was a machine that was something! I watched a boy put in a nickle, and out came a ball of gum. I wanted to try that machine, but all I had in my pocket was a couple of pennies.

I thought about this situation for a while, then I decided to try a penny in the nickle gumball machine. The machine was a great thing, but it wasn't human. Surely a machine couldn't tell the difference between a nickle and a penny. It took someone like Mr. Jenkins at the candy store to tell the difference between nickles and pennies.

So I dropped my penny in the slot and pulled the lever. Know what happened? Nothing. My penny was gone, and I had no gum. Well, I had another penny, so I tried again. The same thing happened. Now two pennies were gone, and I still had no gum.

You may think I wasted my money, but that isn't entirely true. For two cents I learned an important fact of life; two wrongs don't make a right. Now you may be smart enough not to put pennies in a nickle machine, and that's good. But many of us use other methods to try to make two wrongs equal a right.

What do you do if someone hits you? If you're not careful, your first reaction may be to hit back. But is hitting back really going to help? It was wrong of the person to hit you. It would be just as wrong for you to hit him back. Remember the gumball machine and the pennies? Two pennies still did not make the gum come out. Two wrongs do not make a right. But two hits might make a fight.

It's hard to know what to do when someone does something mean to you. Figuring out life's problems is not as simple as merely putting nickles in the nickle machine. But once you know for sure that pennies won't work in the nickle machine, you've come a long way. You've learned that you have to look further for your answers.

You might ask yourself why your friend hit you. Maybe you stepped on his toe. Of course, that doesn't give him the right to hit you, but if you did step on a person's toe, you might resolve to be more careful in the future. And if you accidentally do something to hurt someone, you should make a sincere apology.

People who do things that annoy you usually have their reasons. Life will flow more smoothly if you'll make an attempt to understand the other person's point of view. This week, let's think carefully and try to see the foolishness of dropping pennies into nickle machines.

Sentence prayer: Our Father, help us to see the world from the other person's point of view, at least part of the time. Amen.

PIFFLE AND WHIFFLE

Prop: *A box of miscellaneous items.*

I have a young nephew named Ronald who collects things. Does any of you collect things? What do you collect? (Give time for answers.)

Ron collects all sorts of things. His mother calls his collection piffle and whiffle. Ron finds things others have discarded. People give him things. And he buys more things. And where does all this collection go? Into Ron's room, of course. Finally when most of the space in his room was filled up, Ron's mother told him that something had to go.

Ron took a walk around the block to think, and on this walk he saw a garage sale. That was a new thing to Ron. He thought the garage itself was for sale. A garage was a place all hollow with space. A garage was what he needed. And this one was a bargain. He saw a sign that said 10¢.

Well, Ron plunked his dime down, and he was surprised to learn that he had bought a broken lamp. Right then he learned that a garage sale means that the things *inside* the garage are for sale, not the garage itself.

Ron was disappointed, but it gave him an idea. He

decided to have a garage sale of his own. So he sorted through all things that were crowding his room and saved only the best. The rest he put into his garage sale. At the end of the day, Ron's room was neat, but all up and down the street his playmates' rooms were cluttered with Ron's piffle and whiffle.

Sometimes I think our minds become cluttered with piffle and whiffle. We hear all sorts of ideas at school, at Sunday school, on the playground, at the "Y." Surely all of us need a place all hollow with space where we can sort out useful ideas from useless ideas.

We might pretend to have a garage sale of our minds, keeping the best ideas safely stored in our brains and discarding the useless ideas. It might be hard to decide between useful and useless ideas, but parents and teachers are usually at hand to help with such decisions, if they are consulted.

Some of the good ideas we will want to keep are thoughts of good and beauty and kindness and love. Some useless ideas we should get rid of (and I don't recommend trying to sell them to someone else) are ideas of selfishness, hatred, ugliness, greed. Let's all examine our idea collections once in a while and pare them down until only the very best remain.

Sentence prayer: Our Father, fill our minds with only the best. Amen.

TAKE ME OUT TO THE BALL GAME

Prop: *An assortment of balls.*

Just look at all the balls we have here. Can you tell me what they are? Golf ball. Tennis ball. Basketball. Baseball. Football. Ping-pong ball. Volley ball. (Others if you have them.)

What game do you play with a football? Football, of course. Have you ever tried to play football with a golf ball? People would really laugh at you if you did, wouldn't they? A basketball wouldn't be of much use in a tennis game. Nor would a ping-pong ball be of much use on the baseball diamond. But each ball is good for something.

I often think that people are a lot like balls. They're all good for something. We need them all. We need plumbers and mechanics. We need scientists and teachers. We need politicians and candlestick makers. Doctor, lawyer, merchant, chief. We need them all.

When your sink stops up, whom do you call? The plumber, of course. And are you ever glad to see him when he arrives! When the family car breaks down, whom do you go to? A mechanic. People wouldn't call a lawyer to cure a case of measles or mumps, nor would they call a doctor to teach young people how to read. Like balls that have their specific uses, people have their specific jobs in our world.

Each young person today will have to decide what to do with his or her life. You may get a lot of advice from your family, friends, and teachers, but in the end, you will be the one who has to make the decision. How lucky that is. Decisions are sometimes very hard to make, but how lucky you are to have the opportunity to decide what you will be and do in life.

In olden days many young people had little say about choosing their life's work. Sometimes they were apprenticed to learn a trade, the arrangements being made between the child's parent and the would-be teacher. Thus a child whose talents ran to music and art might be thrust into a life as a clerk or a merchant, and a young person who longed to work with numbers and money might end up mixing paints for an artist.

We should all give thanks that the world has come to recognize the individuality of each person, that we are free to become what we desire to become, and that we are all worthwhile and necessary parts of the universe.

Sentence prayer: Our Father, we thank you for our individuality and for making a place in the world for each of us. Amen.

THOUGHTS ON FAIRY GODMOTHERS

Prop: *A scepter sprinkled with glitter.*

How many of you know what this is? It's a scepter, isn't it? Who uses scepters? Kings. Queens. Who else? What about fairy godmothers? Haven't you all read stories about a fairy godmother with a sparkling scepter?

When does this godmother use her scepter? She uses it when another person is unhappy or in trouble, doesn't she? You may have heard a story about a poor fisherman who couldn't catch fish until the fairy godmother came along and tapped his shoulder with her scepter. After that, fish filled the fisherman's net. Or there's the story of Cinderella, who was unhappy living with her stepsisters and her stepmother. The fairy godmother came along and gave Cinderella a tap with the scepter. Suddenly Cinderella had new clothes and new shoes and a chariot to take her to the ball.

We may think of scepters and fairy godmothers as bits of make-believe found only in fairy tales, but in a way, that's not wholly the case. How would you like to be a fairy godmother? It might be possible, you know. It really might.

For instance, do you know anyone in your school who is sometimes unhappy? Hardly anyone is happy all the time.

And maybe that person has real reason to be unhappy. Have you ever noticed that sometimes everyone picks on a certain person? Or maybe if they don't pick on him, they laugh at him. Or maybe they shun that person and never include him in their plans.

Well, here's an instance where you can play fairy godmother. You can stick up for that person who's being teased or laughed at. Oh, you don't have to cause a scene about it or get into a fight about it. But when you hear other children laughing or poking fun at someone, and if that someone seems unhappy about it, you can pretend that you have a magic scepter. Everyone has some good points, and your job as fairy godmother will be to tap that person's good points with your scepter.

You might say something like, "Oh, Bill's not so bad really. He's always willing to help if you need help and I think that's important." Or you might say, "So what if Ann does brag a little, we all get off the beam sometimes. I think she could be a good friend if we give her a chance."

Your magic scepter will work if you really try to use it. You'll be able to help someone, and you may be surprised to find your classmates saying more nice things about you, too. They'll recognize you as a friendly person and a kind person, and of course you don't need to tell them that you're a fairy godmother with a magic scepter. Let that be your secret.

Sentence prayer: Our Father, thank you for the many ways in which we can make another's life easier. Amen.

BROKEN THINGS

Prop: *A broken cup.*

Do you ever feel sad about broken things? I know I do at times, and I guess that all of you have had the experience of breaking a favorite toy or record or dish. Broken things usually cause sad feelings, and the more important the broken thing is, the sadder the feelings.

If we look around us, we can see broken homes. We can see broken people. We can see broken nations. Sometimes a careful repair job can restore a broken thing, but not always.

One time when I was beachcombing near the sea I noticed all the broken glass that had washed up onto the shore. The glass fragments were unsightly, and they were dangerous to anyone walking barefoot in the sand. Sometimes Scout groups organized patrols that went out and gathered the broken glass and deposited it in trash containers.

Then one day I saw a young boy carefully picking up pieces of the broken glass and placing them in a box. I asked him what he was doing, as he seemed very selective in what he picked up.

"I'm gathering bits of colored glass," he replied. "I'm making a stained-glass window, an art project."

I talked with the boy for a while, and when he was through picking up glass he agreed to show me his project. I went home with him, and he showed me how he laid the shards of glass in a random pattern on a flat surface. Then he melted lead and poured it into the cracks between the pieces of glass, and also around the edges. When the lead hardened, the boy picked up the small glass window he had made. When he held it to the sun it glowed with a rainbow of colors.

I was impressed with that boy's ability to create beauty from destruction, and I think he had a lot to teach all of us. Perhaps nothing is hopelessly destroyed. Perhaps we can salvage the pieces of what was been broken and create something good from them.

(Hold up prop.) I was getting ready to discard this old cup, but I've changed my mind. I've decided to make a planter of it. It will serve well as a holder for an ivy plant. I believe there is hope for all broken things. Perhaps broken homes can be rebuilt. Perhaps the people of broken nations can be reunited. Perhaps broken humans can be rehabilitated and made useful again.

This week, as we look at the broken things in our world, let's try to look at them deeply. Maybe we can be like the boy who salvaged glass chips. Maybe we can learn to create a window—perhaps a window of understanding and brotherhood.

Sentence prayer: Our Father, help us to see new possibilities in all the things around us. Amen.

POCKETS

Prop: *A pair of jeans with at least four pockets.*

How many pockets do you see on these jeans? Four? That's a lot of pockets, isn't it? I like pockets, don't you? Most people do. We have to be careful when we buy jeans. We have to check, or we may be shorted on pockets. Prices are very high these days, and sometimes clothing maufacturers try to save a few cents by eliminating a pocket here and there.

I came home with a pair of jeans the other day, and I was really pleased with them until I started to put my billfold in my hip pocket. Guess what! There was no hip pocket! That sort of ruined that pair of jeans for me right then.

Why do we like pockets so much? Have you ever wondered about that? Why do you like pockets? (Let the children answer.) Okay. We like to have pockets just because they look neat.

What do you carry in your pockets? (Let the children talk.) Money. Toys. Marbles. Snakes. All sorts of treasures. If I asked your mothers what you carry in your pockets, I could probably get another list of treasures that you've forgotten to mention.

We have a rule about pockets at our house. Our rule is that before anyone puts his jeans in the laundry hamper, he must first empty the pockets. Do you have that rule at your house? Have you ever heard the washing machine go CLANK, CLANK, BANG, BANG? Sometimes that happens, and when it does, everyone knows that someone forgot to take the nails or the marbles out of the pockets.

Jeans aren't the only things that have pockets. Did you ever think that you have pockets in your mind? It's true. We do have pockets in our minds, and we have to be very careful about what we store in those pockets.

Sometimes when I meet a person, I can tell just by knowing him a short time what he carries in his mind pockets. Magic? Not at all. If I meet a boy who is all frowns and surly words, I know immediately that the pockets in his mind are filled with gripes and grudges. If someone socked him on the playground a month ago, he remembers it and keeps that resentful memory in a pocket of his mind.

On the other hand, if I meet a girl who is smiling and who has pleasant things to say, I know immediately that the pockets of her mind are filled with love and kindness and goodwill toward others. If someone hit her on the playground a month ago, she would have counted to ten, and then laughed at herself for taking the matter so seriously.

Whenever you stuff things into the pockets of your jeans, think for a moment about the thoughts you stuff into the pockets of your mind. With a little effort, you can fill all your pockets with treasures.

Sentence prayer: Our Father, we thank you for the lasting treasures of life. Amen.

THE SHELL GAME

Prop: *A snail shell or a turtle shell.*

Do you know what this is? Sure. It's a shell. A small animal once lived inside it. Wherever the animal went, it carried this shell with it. This sturdy shell was nature's way of protecting the animal inside from harm.

Just think how handy a shell is for a turtle. If it's raining, all the turtle has to do to stay dry is to pull himself inside his shell. If it's a very hot day, he can protect himself from the sun by pulling his head and feet into the shell. And if a cat or a dog or some other enemy approaches, all the turtle has to do is pull himself inside his shell and wait until the enemy goes away. This usually doesn't take long, because the enemy soon realizes that the turtle can't be reached.

A shell protects a turtle from a lot of pain, but it also prevents him from experiencing a lot of pleasure too. What if he gets hungry? There's nothing to eat inside the shell. He has to come out to experience the pleasure of eating. And the same thing is true if he gets thirsty. He has to come out of the shell to get a drink. And as long as he stays in his shell, he stays in the same place. If he wants to go anywhere, he has to come out of the shell.

Sometimes people are a lot like turtles. People can build shells around themselves to protect themselves from pain. Do you know a person who isn't very good at sports? What does that person do sometimes when the gang suggests a ball game? He may say that he doesn't want to play, that he doesn't like ball games. That person is withdrawing into his shell. If he doesn't play, then he won't be laughed at if he misses the ball, will he? His I-don't-like-to shell protects him.

When I was in grade school, my teacher offered a prize to the person who read the most books. Everyone started reading. The teacher kept a chart of our progress on the bulletin board. Whenever a person made a book report, he got a star by his name. When one girl had about fifteen stars, the rest of us sort of lost interest in the contest. All of a sudden, we didn't like to read. We didn't want to admit that we were being beaten, so we withdrew into our I-don't-like-to shells to protect our feelings.

All of us have shells to some extent. We need shells to protect us from real danger. But we should all remember that to experience the pleasures of life we have to be like the turtle and come out of our shells and take part in the world and its many activities.

This week, if you find yourself saying "I-don't-like-to," ask yourself if you really don't like that certain thing, or if you're just hiding in your shell and missing out on a lot of good times.

Sentence prayer: Our Father, help us to have the courage to enjoy the good things you have provided. Amen.

TOGETHERNESS

Prop: *Handcuffs.*

How many of you know what these things are? Right. They are handcuffs. If I snap one of them around my wrist and then snap the other one around your wrist, the two of us will experience a lot of togetherness—at least until someone unlocks the cuffs and separates us.

A lot has been said in favor of togetherness. We need to be together with our families. We need to spend time with our friends. But sometimes our lives become so filled with togetherness that we suddenly find we have no apartness. In fact, we may reach a point where we become uneasy if we are left alone for any length of time. But aloneness isn't something to be feared and avoided. I believe that much of the important work and the important thinking of the world is done by people when they are alone.

Have you ever heard of Admiral Richard Byrd? Richard Byrd was the first man to fly over the South Pole. He explored in the Antarctic. And he was alone in a hut for months at a time. Worse yet, the hut was buried beneath ice and snow.

Admiral Byrd wanted to study the harsh climate of this

Antarctic region. He was the only person within a hundred miles. Blizzards raged above his hut. Cold numbed his fingers and toes. Sometimes it was eighty degrees below zero outside his hut. And it was dark twenty-four hours a day.

How did Admiral Byrd bear this loneliness? He thought about his plight. He wrote his ideas about life. He thought about the moon and the stars. And he knew that in time, the sun would return. He knew there was order in the universe, and that there was a supreme power behind the order. This power and order gave Richard Byrd hope. He wrote in his diary, "I am not alone."

It is a fact that we cannot always be with people, nor should we want to be. What do you do when you have a cold and have to stay home from school? The day may seem endless if you aren't prepared to deal with solitary time. I think it's a good idea to plan for time to be spent alone. I mean, plan for some time alone in every day. It can be as little as a few minutes, but plan for it and welcome it.

What should you do with such time? Of course that's up to you. You might try reading a special book. Or writing a poem. Or thinking. Or listening to the sounds around you. The world is a wonderful place, and without the distraction of other people, you will be able to discover some of the wonders. And one of the wonders may be the same discovery that Admiral Byrd made when he wrote, "I am not alone." For that is true. No matter how alone you are, God is always with you.

Sentence prayer: Our Father, help us to seek out and enjoy quiet moments with ourselves and with you. Amen.

BROTHER AUGUSTIN'S CLOCK

Prop: *A variety of clocks and watches.*

Can you imagine a world without clocks? What would your home be like without an alarm clock? Without the kitchen clock?

A thousand years ago there were no clocks. You may ask how people could tell what time it was. Many people told time by the sun. People became very good at that method of time-telling. But what did they do on cloudy days? Or what about nighttime?

Brother Augustin, a monk who lived centuries ago, had an unusual method of telling time. A book of psalms was his clock. Brother Augustin lived in a monastery. He was a bellringer. He had to wake   his brothers for prayers at three o'clock in the morning. How do you suppose he knew the time?

In the evening Brother Augustin would begin to read his psalms. He kept track of the pages he read. When he finished a certain number of pages, he would jump up and run to the church belfry and ring the bell.

Brother Augustin told time by the number of psalms he read. But sometimes this plan failed. Once he fell asleep.

When he woke up, the sun was high, and his superior scolded him for falling asleep. Brother Augustin needed a better way to tell time, but his Bible was his only clock.

It's hard to imagine what our world would be like without clocks. Have you ever thought of how much of your life is regulated by clocks? A lot of it, that's for sure. Most of us get up by the clock. We know we have just so much time in which to dress and eat breakfast and get to school or work.

You know that once you're at school, your day is still ruled by the clock. Each class lasts so many minutes, then there's recess, lunch hour, more classes. Sometimes we may feel that we are slaves to the clock. Yet we would not want to go back to using sundials or rely on the reading of psalms to count the minutes and hours.

I think one of the most important things to realize about time is that it is a gift given equally to everyone. We all have exactly the same amount of hours in each day. Rich people don't receive twenty-six hours a day and poor people don't receive twenty-one hours. We all get an even twenty-four hours to work with. How we use our time is not always up to us. There are certain required things that must be done, but each of us has at least a few minutes, or perhaps hours, during the day that are ours to do with as we please.

This week, as you start each day, think about your special gift of time. God has given you twenty-four hours. What are you going to do with them?

Sentence prayer: Our Father, help us learn to use our time wisely, to benefit ourselves and others. Amen.

TEN-SPEED

Prop: *A picture of a bicycle.*

How many of you know how to ride a ten-speed bike? I grew up riding an ordinary one-speed bike, and I was really surprised when I tried out a friend's new ten-speed. I had heard him talk a lot about his bicycle. He was always telling me how easy it was to ride up hills on it.

When I actually got on the bike, I liked it well enough. It sped along on level ground very easily, but when I came to my first hill, I was disappointed. Going up the hill didn't seem as easy as my friend had said it would be. In fact, I was huffing and puffing and making hardly any progress at all.

"Shift into a lower gear," my friend called to me. "You've got more power there if you'll just learn to use it."

So I managed to shift to a more powerful gear, and I made it up the hill fairly easily. Afterward, I thought a lot about what my friend had said. Unknowingly he spoke a great truth when he said, "You've got more power there if you'll just learn to use it." You may ask where this power is. Maybe you don't feel very powerful at all. Some days I feel that way, too. But the potential power is in our bodies, and it's in our thoughts.

Before we speak a word, we have to think of that word. Before we do any action, we have to have the thought of the action in our minds. Nothing in our lives happens unless a thought precedes it. Thoughts are the most powerful things in our lives, so it follows logically that we must be very careful in our choice of thoughts. Notice I said in our *choice*. For this is the all-important word. We do have a choice of the thoughts that we think.

If we think good and positive thoughts, our lives will follow good paths. But if we think negative thoughts, we may be letting ourselves in for trouble. Now and then gloomy thoughts come to all of us—fears, jealousies, hatred, selfishness, and many others. Maybe we can't keep these thoughts from coming, but we can be conscious of them and get rid of them as quickly as possible. We can't keep unpleasant thoughts from entering our minds, but we can keep them from making themselves at home there.

It is very important for each of us to fill our minds with great thoughts, because we will never rise higher than the things we think about. A person can literally think his way to success, if he holds successful thoughts in his mind and backs them up with work and faith.

Whenever you see a ten-speed bicycle, remember that we all have more power than we realize. Put your thoughts in gear, and support them with faith and work.

Sentence prayer: Our Father, thank you for the great power that lies in our thoughts, and help us to use this power in the best way. Amen.

THE WHITE ELEPHANT

Prop: *A white elephant figurine or some other completely useless article.*

Have you ever heard someone say, "I don't want that thing. It's a white elephant"? If you've heard that expression, you may have wondered what it meant. I heard an interesting story that will help explain the expression.

In far-off India, Ali and his father, Japur, hunted elephants. One day they caught one in their trap. "A white elephant!" Ali exclaimed. "He looks very special."

They fed the elephant, treated it kindly, and led it home. News of the white elephant spread. People came from miles around to see it and to bring food for it. But soon the newness wore off, and the crowd quit coming.

Japur said, "The elephant must work." He took the white elephant to the forest where he planned for it to carry timbers with its strong trunk. But immediately an angry crowd gathered.

"White elephants never work," the crowd shouted. "Bad luck!"

Japur tried to sell the elephant. But nobody wanted an elephant that couldn't work.

"I have an idea," Ali smiled. "Each year we take the maharaja a gift. Let's give the maharaja this white elephant."

Japur nodded. "Only a maharaja can afford a white elephant. Working people need working elephants."

So Ali and Japur went to the palace, and the maharaja welcomed his gift. Servants prepared feasts, and many people came to see the white elephant. But Ali and Japur hurried home. They laughed. They were rid of their burden. As time passed, they made jokes. They called any useless item a white elephant.

How would you like to have a white elephant? Not many of us would. Oh, it would be a novelty for a while. People would come to see it. But then what? What would we do with it after the novelty wore off? We'd wish we were rid of it, and there might not be a maharaja handy to give it to.

In today's language, a white elephant can be anything that is useless, and this can include people. Do you know any people who are white elephants? People who have never worked? People who do not do their share of the chores? People who belong to a group but do not help with the work could be called white elephants. We all need to examine our lives and make sure that we are not white elephants at home, at school, or in any club we belong to.

Sentence prayer: Our Father, we give thanks that you have chosen us to help do the work of the world. Amen.

SHOOTING STARS

Prop: *A cardboard star.*

I had an uncle who grew up in Kansas in the 1930s, when the land was suffering from heat and drouth. This was before the days of air conditioning, and sometimes it was literally too hot to sleep at night. On those hot sleepless nights, my uncle would take a blanket and spread it on the ground in his backyard. He told me once that he really enjoyed those sweltering nights because he saw many shooting stars, and he was impressed with the beauty of the night.

I thought of this when my own children were young, and I realized that they had never seen the sky at night. We had daylight saving time where we lived, and sometimes it was light until after nine o'clock, which was past the children's bedtime. So one night I wakened them and took them outside at midnight. It was August, and we were treated to a display of shooting stars that they have never forgotten.

I've heard a story about Abraham Lincoln and shooting stars. Once Lincoln was visiting at the home of a farmer. This friend happened to be up in the middle of the night, and he looked out the window and saw many shooting stars.

He had never seen anything like it before. He wakened Lincoln and told him the world was coming to an end, that all the stars were falling.

Abraham Lincoln took a look outside and reassured the farmer. He told him to go back to bed, that there might be shooting stars, but that the great constellations would still stand.

I always remember that thought whenever I see a shooting star. The great constellations still stand. It's a comforting thought. We may experience a lot of shooting stars in our lifetime, bright flashes that end in nothing, that disappear from sight even as we watch.

We plan for a picnic—and then it rains. For a while the picnic was like a shooting star in our minds, but then the rain came, and the picnic and the star both disappeared. We plan to go to summer camp—and we get the mumps. We save money to buy a special gift—and the store raises the price.

Everyone has had the experience of seeing his bright plans end in disappointment. But the world still turns. The great constellations still stand. The next time you are disappointed in your plans, remember Abraham Lincoln and the shooting stars. Shooting stars make a beautiful and awesome sight, but when they're gone, you still have the universe God created, and God is always with you to steady you along your way. The great constellations still stand.

Sentence prayer: Our Father, we give thanks for this universe in which we live, and for the good you have provided for us. Amen.

WHAT AN IMAGINATION!

Prop: *A wheel.*

How often have you heard someone say, "It's just your imagination," or "You're letting your imagination run away with you"? Statements like these may lead you to believe that imagination is something to be on guard against, when just the opposite may be true.

What is imagination? I like to think of it as picturing something in the mind. Anything that happens, anything that is invented, any great plan, first has to be pictured in the mind. The person who invented the wheel first pictured a wheel in his mind. Imagination!

If you want something that you don't have, one sure way to get it is to picture it, or imagine it, in your mind, then work toward making your mental picture come true.

How many of you have heard of Benjamin Franklin? You may have heard about his experiments with electricity and kites, but Benjamin Franklin was also a businessman, and he was a famous American statesman. But before he was any of these, he was an unknown writer.

When he was young, Ben worked at making candles, and his family laughed at his idea of being a writer. But his older brother published a newspaper, so Ben used his imagination. He wrote short articles. Of course he didn't tell anyone he was writing. Instead, he waited until the family was asleep at night, then he slipped from bed and ran to his brother's printing office. He shoved his articles under the door, unsigned. Then he ran back home and got into bed.

Ben's brother liked the articles and printed them. Ben still didn't tell anyone that he had written the articles. He just enjoyed seeing them in print, and he enjoyed hearing his family talk about them.

Years later, Benjamin Franklin wrote *Poor Richard's Almanac.* It was a small pamphlet filled with unusual facts and wise proverbs. Some of those proverbs are still famous today. A penny saved is a penny earned. A small leak will sink a large ship. It is hard for an empty bag to stand upright.

Ben sold his almanac for a few cents. Some copies of it have been saved to this day, and they are preserved in libraries. They are so valuable they cannot be bought for any price.

Ben Franklin used his imagination. He imagined himself as a writer, then he worked to make his pictured image come true. Each of you can do that, too. Everyone has an imagination. Decide what it is that you really want from your life. Keep a strong picture of this desire in your imagination. Then work toward achieving whatever it is that you want. You'll be surprised what the combination of imagination and hard work can do for you. Try it and see.

Sentence prayer: Our Father, thank you for our minds and for the wonderful and mysterious ways in which they work. Amen.

HAPPINESS

Prop: *A sign saying Happiness.*

I think adults sometimes mistakenly believe that all children are happy and carefree. You people don't have to pay taxes. You don't have to worry about repairing the roof on your house or the leaks in the basement. And the grocery bill is no problem for you. But according to what I hear from teachers, children are not happy all the time.

In fact many of you are unhappy a lot of the time. Now whether you feel that you are happy or unhappy most of the time, most of you would like to be happier. Isn't that right?

When I asked a teacher what children worry about, what makes them unhappy, she had a long list of answers. It seems that children worry about grades. They worry about whether or not the other children like them. They worry about things they hear their parents worrying about. And so it goes.

There's no sure formula for happiness. Each person has to learn to find happiness in his own way. But a wise man named Dale Carnegie once had some ideas on happiness that I'd like to tell you about. Mr. Carnegie's advice to unhappy people was to think of all the things that they value and that they now have. He advised them to actually make a list of them. I won't ask you people to make a list right now, but maybe you'll want to make one later. For now, just make a mental list of the things you have that you really value.

Who wants to name some of the things on his list? (Let the children speak.) Yes, you value your homes, your families, your brothers and sisters, your toys, your pets, your bicycles. Why, there is an endless list of things you have that you really value, isn't there?

The next step of Mr. Carnegie's plan was to imagine that all these things were taken away from you. Wow! That would be awful. But imagine it if you can. No home. No family. No brothers and sisters. No toys. No pets. No bicycles. No TV. Everything is gone. Wiped out. How would you feel if that happened to you? You'd feel pretty glum, wouldn't you? Well, we won't think about that for too long.

The third part of Mr. Carnegie's plan was to imagine that everything you valued, and that had been taken from you, was given back to you. Can you imagine how happy you'd feel? Think about that. Imagine it!

Now think about this. You already have all those things right now, so why not be happy right now? It's a good question. Why not be happy right now?

Sentence prayer: Our Father, thank you for the everyday blessings that we sometimes take for granted. Help us to realize their value and give thanks. Amen.